Threefer

Threefer

ein threefer pour vous?

Ken Bolton

PUNCHER & WATTMANN

First published in 2013
Published by Puncher and Wattmann
PO Box 441
Glebe NSW 2037
http://www.puncherandwattmann.com
puncherandwattmann@bigpond.com

National Library of Australia
Cataloguing-in-Publication entry:

Bolton, Ken
Threefer

ISBN 9781922186461

I. Title.
A821.3

Cover design by Matthew Holt
Printed by McPhersons Printing Group

This project has been assisted by the Australian Government through the Australia Council, its arts funding and advisory body.

Australia Council
for the Arts

for Julie and Crab,
Anna and Chris

I

Footprints   1

II

London Postcard   31
The Funnies   32
On Reflection   34

III

Some Days   49

Footprints

limbs, moving through the air,
as cool about them

        as an almost liquid medium

    #

    days
of not writing poems, & at nights
especially

    #

above the trees   there is no
mystery.   There is
just the plane   it is crawling slowly along the
sky .   like a fly along the rim of a lampshade

Wayne Shorter

          'Footprints' – live

I rub Cath's
beautiful shoulder

I rub

the other, too—

(Also beautiful)

the cat
is here again, coming up the ladder to the loft

to butt my chin, with its head,
purring, like a small
enamoured
tractor

a little fridge

I am that least admirable
of Men
I always give up boundless love.
now, all I
can think
is of your nether lip, your entirely
strong & specific nervous face
& the
salty
briny brown which I associate with your lips, &
with your skin
which seems

2

                                                        (the cat, a head-

butter for love)

            the secret river that runs like a moon through
            girls.

                        the obvious river,
                  that runs (like ...

            the running of the bulls at Pamplona

                        The nun's story.

now in the afternoon   with you   it is you I love   in the afternoon
light.

what's the name of the feeling I have about you that says
you should be in a book   & illustrating the easy life that comes
of never singing out loud but going round always singing in your
                  head & thinking there
            also ?

                  •

                  relaxing lying-back

                        calm & pale   as a cigarette that is smoked,

lying here   am

           I smoking one, aren't I?

"In dreams begin responsibilities"

(") responsibilities

           start in bed"   you hardly seem

              •

             … as I run the …

         •

sliding down the page
      I translate
a french poem. I've
washed my hair.

        •

      as if we would live forever?

         Yes, as if we would!

    Philip Whalen, a book of drawings by Kirchner,

       Street Scenes of Berlin,

           the veiled, the hawkish figures

And Etta James is dead.

Late at night
reading Ted

—*Ted* is dead
                    (*and* Tod)—
                    und Tod

                                        yep, him too

the terrific days of summer

                    already   the sun is making the pool rooms
in the British Lion   too hot in the afternoon   or soon will,
& the carpet stinks of beer again

                                        & parties have begun   - Colin's
        got a job til Xmas

                    #

        a house you lived in
                    & another

        #

                                        the last you had begun to be
                    the luckiest   the toaster might catch that sun

5

every morning, & near it the knife, when you get up
after every night. —marmalade, or crumb; the toasty cat
at its sour white plate, your jeans undone.
lemons.

 #

the air   risks itself among her hair   & everything

 is aroused

the air   & things   are all aroused & everything, & that.

it was like   some sort of   'stuff'

 #

 : "Art"?

 : there is none : love is artless.   There is only
      the wallpaper,

  & the chintz & carpet

 •

 A chint?
 (My kingdom for one!)

 •

                    the fabulous limp calligraphy of the
afternoon

spiritual miles distant from the thought of you

we will be passing the telephone booths soon
& then we will be in the suburbs, things that say
'COKE' against the sky

          —I'll
just open the car door   & get a bit of fresh air & stare

... above the booth, resting.

                    sky   cloud   chimney   aeroplane

      the record player has not been on for hours
      though the light on the record player glows

      but the intense sad notes still 'haunt' the air
      & affect the view, out through the bars,

      of the street & the factory across the road

      with their own grid, of wire & bars,
      on all their windows, staring back

      the sunday traffic, occasionally, roaring past

      I get up, & put on Lou Reed's
      'Rock n Roll', which I love. It always makes the bars

seem more *neutrally* rigorous—

how I'm beginning to feel now.

lists of adjectives for days
                    : terrific days,
                      inelegant days,
                      eloquent days, days
                      like spring & days
                      like summer,
                      impenetrable days
                      literal days
                      the saddest days,
                      days that are stoical, classical or cool

the effect of Donald Brook
the effect of Nigel Roberts.
the effect of Forbes,   (the effect
                              of taking all their personal
                                                     effects   &
nailing them to a board   & comparing them

& of thinking   how **that**, in effect,
                              was like summer;
                                                        the
       effect

of looking at the city

                          & knowing

you could / *be* there.

           like your chest is full of brows

                                     suddenly / ceasing

to frown, now smiling.

          days/
               without parallel,
                & days, days & days of them, that are all
                                      exactly –

the – same

                •

          days   without parallel,

       of)
              let's go sleeping

            #

there's the air   risking itself   among her hair

   aroused

    & things

  & everything, & that.

        #

The Paris Commune

    Manet O'Hara Coltrane
          Puvis de Chavannes, in Glebe.
          In Bega!

—& the loons, like de Chirico—the Germans, Kirchner
Kokoschka, Adorno—Christa Wolf.

        #

'hermetic' days .
New photo-realist days

the sort of thing   that for some people, presumably,
is conjured by a lawnmower ad on television

                  Pam laughs

         is it really effortless? is it
         really so smooth & green?

Tonight I'm 'high'

'where I write at night & think of you'

where I aim my best ideas

     (like
        "Everything is Kafka"

       Like, "everything

                 is, like, ..."   & so on   )

            #

       the joint kicks in

   #

                where am I?
                    adrift again?

The *British Lion* is opening its doors

Reification   can be my tool too, & come in handy!

Midget legends of our time

I feel like a temple must feel
                              a feeling temple

The phrase "Italian Drink"

                    nearly abstract nearly real,

          & Wayne Shorter—'live'

                                        … like

(which is where I stand)

(& sometimes laugh, sometimes (almost) cry)

              ideas for poems float past

      (&)

              For a second, not even looking up
I feel like a temple without a saint

                    My life,

— "Mate, pull up a pew!" —

where so often …

There is no truth

There is tearfulness

Rather than

tragedy

A pew is pulled up

a terrible mildness

Do I have my 'sights'

'set'

on something

that is Universal

(without feeling like Elmer Fudd,

or a Greek athlete?)

do I?

'Masquelero'

#

I put on, again, 'Footprints'

\#

a book of drawings by Kirchner, Philip Whalen

the Berlin Street Scenes,

The Paris Commune

Manet   Coltrane   O'Hara

—& the loons: de Chirico—the Germans, Kirchner
(Kokoschka, Adorno—Christa Wolf)

Filippo De Pisis

& at nights
especially

days writing poems

my limbs
move through the air
(cool about them
as   )

living brilliantly

•

indigently

•

An "Italian Drink", nearly abstract nearly real, like
my best ideas

comes thru the window

#

which is where I stand

& laugh, (or cry),

& where abrasively

& beautifully

ideas for poems float past

I can write

telling another poet
how I love.

#

but I do not write
I do not tell
(I am running,

responsibly, the ...)

#

I am that least admirable of men

#

having an italian drink, at a window
with a pillow under my arm

                          & the salty
briny brown which I associate with your lips,

with your skin,
                      loony also

#

on the other hand :

Do I have my 'sights'
                  'set'
               on something
that is Universal

Like Errol Flynn,

an ageing Errol
— & the twins —
in
The Big Boodle ?

today,
aflame with love for you my main
feeling is un-nameable   & is concerned with the way

these attitudes, which you weave about you, you weave
about you.

#

Let me play
with your poodle

(Old Saying)

comes 'thru the window'

(Thank you, Tampa.)

#

now in the afternoon
  in the afternoon light.
it is you I love

#

what's the name of the feeling I have about you that says
you should be in a book   (you should illustrate the easy life
                                    that comes

of ...

this makes you mysterious

little white Magrittes
against the quiet, loud blue

(&)

For a second, not even looking up
I feel like a temple without a saint

My life, where so often ...

I'm a just luv luv luv you, baby
I'm a just keep on luvving you

(as, so often, McKinley
Morganfield had
cause to iterate)

Sigh!
(a terrible mildness)

(Thank you, Chet Baker.)

& isn't it
better here, living
now?

18

Is everything 'Kafka'?

Is anything?

The *British Lion* is opening its doors

              true

          (but I am not their doorman)
I am running the bulls at Pamplona.

Reification can be my tool too

Midget legends
          of our time

I feel like a temple must feel
relaxing lying-back

              #

"I know what he *did* have his eyes on—'nominally'"

             (—Raoul Walsh)

         #
the record player has not been on for hours
         #

you have 'pulled up a pew', a
mental pew

you 'sit there'
in your mental pyjamas

#

though the light on the record player glows
the intense sad notes still 'haunt' the air —

& affect the view, out through the bars
of the street & the factory across the road

with their own grid, of wire & bars,
on all their windows, staring back

Who could like
temples & churches?
In truth you never have.

the sunday traffic, occasionally, roaring past

I get up, & put on Lou Reed
which I love.

neutrally rigorous bars—which is

how I'm beginning to feel now,
like one of the bars, on the window.

o, to be one of those !

whose teeth
bump those of the men they kiss
wondrously   girls with fingers, girls in clinches

the secret river that runs like a moon

how **that**, in effect,

                                        was like summer;
                               is like summer)

                                                                    &

the
     effect
of looking at the city

                              —   A perspective view   —

          where
                  above the trees   there is no
          mystery.

            just the plane   crawling slowly along the
          sky   (like a fly along the rim of a lampshade)

          like your chest is full of brows

                                          suddenly / ceasing
to frown, now smiling.

                              Your name is Rembrandt,
                              Paul Rembrandt?

Have a banana—no?
a roll-mop then!

Write to Sal;

Draw my hand

Floyd Jones   ('Playhouse Down')

Hullo, Akira!

Viv!

Susan Mervyn-Jones

#

Monsieur Paul Sloan, master

#

exult ,   exultant

"Friend or foe," says the cook
in this establishment

he is
a 'joker'

an establishment I today had my lunch in
or, anyway, coffee

days/
         without parallel,

Now,
Big swigs of resin / retsina
The joint kicks in —
    there goes my handwriting —

                              memories
                                        (& dreams)

    of)
         let's go sleeping

                              the last you had begun to be
         the luckiest   the toaster the sun
         every morning, & near it the knife, when you get up
         after every night. —marmalade, or crumb; the toasty cat
         at its sour white plate, your jeans undone.

    Lemons

         *

hermetic days .

B: "Art"?

"Shall I place your bags in the vestibule, SUH?!"

days
which the art
in our mind makes

.   Juan Gris,   Jack Benny,   Frank Stella

like paintings
—like *the Piano Lesson*,
like Braque!   & terrific days
                like Jackson Pollock

        —& the loons like de Chirico, Konrad Bayer—
:   Kirchner
                        Kokoschka, Adorno

                        Christa Wolf
                                        loony
    also

    if you've got some change
            & you want to make that phone call
            (make it)

lists of adjectives for days

              -

            list begins

            list ends

            stoical, classical or cool

       on a Japanese envelope: *This letter may contain no*
                      message
            ha ha ha — & many hardly do

                *

the fabulous limp calligraphy of the afternoon

spiritual miles distant

           the 'obvious' river, that runs,
             like a bull, thru …
      *

the terrific days of summer
are here again,
          already   the sun is making the pool rooms
in the British Lion
            too hot in the afternoon

the carpet stinks of beer again

parties have begun

the air   risks itself
                              & everything

the air   & things   are all aroused & everything, & that.

It was like   some sort of   'stuff'.

                              *

Tonight I'm 'high'

                                        & where there is a sense of
        forever

        (where I write at night & think of you)
                                        where I aim my best
        ideas

Awake & Refreshed
tho with nothing on the page!

two thirds of a second,

Archie Shepp   Lou Reed   Fats Waller

            I put on, again, Wayne Shorter — it is
                        'Footprints' - live

#

—maintaining altitude—

4 or 5 short blacks & retsina chasers

#

the music, then, is Coltrane—Coltrane 'live' in Europe,
        courtesy of Crab

    "Four stars, Ken!   Any biscuits?"
        as the dog said, coming in

.   put-in-my-place.
                                        But what has done this?

        Coltrane? Europe?
)

        my friends—whom I sail 'by', 'beneath', 'between'
Mary, Mill, Craig, Coltrane & Pepper Adams — *or*
Cecil Payne, if it was him—
                        Frank O'Hara

Pam, Laurie, the big brains line up

(&)
there's
the photo of Mill —

        'A Step Away From Them'

and a photo of The Banana—
  easing herself, nimbly, off the
      trampoline,
  where she had been sitting, cross-legged

II

London Postcard

A Quiet Morning At The Wapping Project

'Avenue Victor Hugo, cognac—
Lianne Fowler as Isabel,' the caption says.
And continues: *'A French Picture Show'.* So a movie still
I expect. Why such an image will
anchor one. Benediction. One is blessed.

It is the softness of the tones
& of the outlines—the slight rose of the flesh,
the mint cool of the T-shirt, planes
of cheek, forehead, & arms—hands
twisted beneath her chin, pressed

against her mouth—echoing, I suppose, our
own anxieties, resolving them
in an image of beauty, a balm
of solipsism & objectivity, of calm
& pity—for ourselves—selves we mend

with this distance & identification.
'The fictive life of the tourist'? Or would
I feel this way about this image
anywhere? Lianne Fowler gauging something—
something within or without—tense, paying attention.

I attend to her in the idle moment. Not a film, it turns out,
but the exhibition of a story-boarded graphic novel, an
exercise in 'so funky, so French!'. Corn.
Still, I liked the photograph.

The Funnies

The comics were best kept simple—
The Little King, Boofhead, Brenda Starr.
The King never spoke
& others spoke 'but briefly'
in his presence—announcing
something—this or that—
& the King would leap,
scowl or shrug,
exclamation mark
above his head.
I understood him
from an early age.
The cartoonist's
ineptitude
was essential: Boofhead's
Egyptian style
of ambulation,
his Egyptian surprise.
"The true archaic simplicity"
as someone might have said.
Arms akimbo, one leg lifted,
mouth open, his eyes—did I
ever see him sleep?—pools
of black.
The amateurish, confident
styling of Brenda Starr.
Where is that world now?
I wanna go there & roll
cigarettes, roll my own
smokes, as Dan Hicks

had it—later, in a more
sophisticated age—
an age that
looks back—
at the King affronted,
Boofhead flummoxed, or
Boofhead stymied,
Starr crying or
having a thought ...
looks back, looks back,
astonished at that innocence.

On Reflection

for Ruth Fazakerley

I will have spent
half of my life on this street

that I like
                but that I never
pay attention to

                I think I don't
want its image fixed
too unchangeably

                It has
that combination of bland & bleak
I like
                & bits
                        —sections—
have a different character
from the whole

                perhaps there is no whole
                        no single Hindley Street

Nothing over two stories pretty much except
at either end—

lots of sky.

I used to ride in from West Terrace in
the early 90s, *five days a week*—

                                      the ugly end,
that has got even uglier,
tho its resolutely charmless sequence

of takeaway food, closed businesses, *Canadian Lodge*,
give it character. Unkempt, un-cared for.
                                            No foot traffic.

The bowling alley amuses—

fifties-sixties moderne, curved roof, wall surfaced
with some material featuring

mica or crushed glass.
The sparkle that will entice. Better, the

electricity sub-station, so out of place
in the centre of a town. Genuinely amusing.

                Hindley seems suspended

between the two relative higher points:
the West Terrace end & the King William.

                                      I like
especially
                 the middle, either
side of the Greek chemist

                            #

which

reminds me of a Hopper streetscape
I knew—Mexican-looking, I
always thought, tho probably it isn't—

#

& where the lovely,
anomalous *Star Grocery*—Greek, blue-&-
white—was,

on the corner of Morphett,

like something in an Australian
country town

but now, at last, gone

The King William St end
consists of a flow—

people sluice in & out, via Hindley,
past various retail snares—

from King William and nearabouts—
to disappear into the railway station—

or they gobble food & go.

#

(A different
demographic.)

#

This is not the real Hindley St.

•

The *Star Grocery,*

replaced by the awful *Hog's Breath,*
which lasted a year or so & closed,

where now there is a twenty-four hour
convenience store. *Like a country town*

in another country—India?—how long
will this last?
    There is one—'conveniently'—
almost every hundred yards.
      Innocuous enough,
there are about three I sometimes go to,
not very regularly,

on the basis of what they stock: some
don't sell nuts. Some papers, some …
         (etc)
In each case they're broke I expect tho maybe not
(one is forging ahead)

Across the road is the hotel, one of the five
or six. I've seen awful things happen there

A crazed bikie head-butted his girlfriend
outside this one on a busy Friday or Saturday night

She fell instantly. I remember the crowd kept moving—
He was too violent to deal with.

The street feels both intimate & pleasantly wide,

The traffic moves slowly for the most part
& you can step off the curb into it

pretty much as you like, unless you actually *have*
a death wish—& then, why not if that's how you
feel?

                                        •

(In which case, Morphett Street or the West Terrace end
is the place to go.)

                                        •

        In the coffee shop yesterday
as I was reading & thinking—in my

                                agenda-less,
'some-call-it-thought' mode—
                                I heard
a voice say "Stan Brackhage"

How amusingly high-art & avant-garde &
shorthand for—well, whatever Stan stood for.

Or what he now has been boiled down to mean

(I've seen half an hour or so of
nothing-happening & was not impressed:

give me earlier more German film
or give me Cassavetes or Fassbinder

                                or even Woody Allen

                                    or visual art (LeWitt,
Hesse, Smithson)

                                    •

                        a film festival is being organized,
or so I think—

                                            •

                        I hadn't realized the arts-powerful
were at the next table

                                tho, in various combinations,
they do come here a bit

                                the 'arts-powerful'

a phrase coined, on the model of
David Kerr's "the art-interested"

                                        one I
always loved

                                •

                        Now we just say "punter"
                                •
tho I know the Australia Council expressly said
somewhere, that we shouldn't use the term

a bunch of people like—well, no,
exactly like—a Houyhnhnm Commintern—

small-minded, *noble*, idiotic

                        #

                        I like the light
here

I like, I think, the way
                                    it's not
a shopping street: people move mostly on it

—amble, lope, trudge & bounce along—

casually to a pub, to TAFE or Uni, or to get
to some other part of town
                                              someone
goes by on a skateboard

                                girls wander
talking
            in pairs, students

                        —the permanent
feminine conversation that establishes the limits
& shape of normalcy, what is real,
                                          &
                        "*the Idiot Dreams
Of Men*" :

            like mine

                        Or are they more often
similar?
            More than I think?
                                it was a woman who said
"Stan Brakhage" this morning

                                —its valency
having changed for me

changed in my estimation

for now.

Tho for why for now?—

                              meaning
her thoughts focus on the same things
as mine do

        (Eva Hesse
                Rainer Werner Fassbinder—

to use them   as counters, tokens
                     things

skipping constantly between existing
in their own right

               & as ideas, signs
        •
I think the Marxist term, once,
was "reified"
            •
          Tho the Australia Council
has probably ruled that term out of count, off-
bounds

       at least 'for a funded oeuvre'

           #

"You do want to be funded, don't you, buddy?"

#

For Communism — No banana!

Who, decorative, *did*

Zeus appear to   as

'a shower of gold' ?

— ('funding') —

Some Baroque

bint

(in Rembrandt, Gentileschi)

(in Klimt & in the

film of the Henry James novel

Wings Of A Dove?

with beautiful Helena Bonham-Carter)

#

Are We

In VENICE Now?

#

No, I'm pressing the button

for the lights

& leaning here, with the mail—

quite a lot of it this morning

envelopes & boxes

& waiting for the traffic to stop

so I can

cross Morphett St & go to work.

(really go to work)

The LAC,
whose grandiosity as a name
                              is made to fade
by the sculpted lion that represents it & stands
looking out to the Adelaide Cricket Ground, or the
shunting yards of the railway,
                    where they're about to build a hospital,
                              moodily heroic
reminding of all that is passed
                              the 1950s, the
British Empire
            a world that was simpler,

                              the avant-garde?

Has the avant-garde passed?   Someone ask the Arts Council.
What is the responsible view?

                    The clouds that gather
behind the lion
                    that gather almost as if
his profile required them,
                    massed, & 'beautiful', if sad—

bland, bleak, Turneresque

            That old bore
                              give me
one of the other great names instead
                              almost any
will do

Dufy, Picasso

    Gerhard Richter

maybe not Stan Brakhage

(A Turner painting—*The Lion Arts Centre, sunset,*
storm approaching,
    ink & watercolour, 2012.)

      Hindley Street
doesn't even shrug

    —at these names, these meanings—

even to appeal (like a street in Paris), *Am I*
not more beautiful?

    (Than Stan, than Raoul, than Gerhard
would depict?)
    Hindley Street doesn't
in fact hear or notice

      •

    Like a man in a t-shirt &
jeans
  & on his feet, thongs—
      cigarettes
folded into the sleeve of his shirt—

      concerned
with something more practical

      some dream more
earthbound

—rent, the body's well-being—

A student I know
                    goes past, I register &
say hullo
                    his mind, like his girlfriend's,
less concerned with reification

                                        •

                                living

in-the-moment

                              •

                    — as I did,
                              a moment ago.

Now the traffic prepares to slow
                              slows & stops
& I go to work.
                              #
            I always knew this would happen
                              #
                    Danae — that is
the name. Money for love.

                              #

            "punter, punter, punter"

                              #

& as I arrive there is a punter right there—
Ruth, waiting to buy some Foucault

III

Some Days

the balmy nougat walls   & out the windows
the harbour   the city lined up like rows of electrical appliances —

transistors — shining bright cubes
in the late afternoon sun   against the blues of Balmain-Rozelle harbour

& the sky — the containers,
stretched, paled   like daubs along the water. the tugs.

nearer, on the verandah, the cats   grey   orange

                        *

                        humming a line
from an advertisement,
                        watching a lizard in the grass.

        "She's the only one
          can write about her
          broken radio & not
          be self conscious,"
                        Kerry said once.

                #

"It's great being drunk all day"

                (on the other hand)   *"What's so good about it?"*

                        #

(& went

inside).

#

glum suddenly

suddenly tired

*

Intriguing Reasons

The Meaning Of Paintings

Great phrases

*

a factory on the way to Rae's place
with a Dickensian title — "Bleakly Gray
(Pty Ltd)".

Surely one

'we all find funny'

*

I'm walking now, amongst my old
friends, the hills (witnesses I think
to so much of my past life.

Hmm,

the hills have reminded me
of modern australian poetry, the kind

Les writes
(Very Depressing),

…   'adult' life: the kind of thing
you find,

in the poetry of Lowell, & those poets.

poets like that

*

"But the making of poems,

as against (*what?*)

versified opinions & illustrative moral
tales, means the deliberate choice & creation of limits"

Does it?

Doo dee-doo do-doo

(*Very* depressing?)

*

August 12th

The reading next day
went the same way. Very small audience.
Every reader in gloom. Apparently it
"all sounded very good."

             *

gripping the iron bar of Hellenism

             *

                              At night you write
while someone

                    etc

                                        while someone breathes

(while someone eats & breathes,   & is looking out the window).

        vamping here   & vamping there

I'm learning how they live from books.

We are writing Ten Facts In The City.

outside, actually, the jackhammers drill, in what
looks like 'heat'—but I can't hear them in the quiet I have
created, with a live tape   playing very loud the
Rolling Stones.

every now & then we assume it has happened, that
some man has gone beserk & is knocking down pieces of the
stage, pushing into them & tearing them down & stepping
over them, pieces of scenery fallen all about

                                                every now & then

but it never happens

                    *

                    There, I've said it, in all its
simpleness — the best teacher lives outside, the best
teacher lives inside you, beating blood, breathing
air, the best teacher is alive.

                              'is an olive'?

the terrific drifting of the day

                    *

John approached Kerry in the University Cafeteria & said you're Kerry Leves,
aren't you? My name's John Forbes. And he asked him if he was writing any poetry
lately. Kerry said yes & no. He was, but he wasn't happy with it, & he said that he
hadn't been feeling very real lately. What? said Forbes. Well, you know, how
sometimes you just don't feel very real? & John fled.

We talk about the cat & chickens on the grass

       *

             morning,
or afternoon. for a moment you are in
yesterday.
       but you remember.
              briefly,
you play a game: you test your hunger to see
if, by that, you can tell:
          you go
to the window to see if the waves
are rolling in
       as they did yesterday.

below, along the beach, the waves
are rolling in.
         downstairs a radio play
begins.

       *

             I put
the oranges in the pocket
of the duffle coat I use as a spread
& get in on the red sheets close
        enough to sleep
to not be kept awake by their pallid slight
stickiness
& dream "o, leopard skins, jungles, o
        the cream we use as lubricant, Jane. Jane, take down

those
leopard skin undies. The main thing I want to do

(jungle drums)

*

" in Australia

as I have been these last 25 minutes... "

*

there are
some postcards — three of a Bonnard
(*Woman with a Cat*, 1912) with its beautiful
lemon yellow third of table which
reminds me of my poem "lemons".
there is a copy of "lemons" fixed there, to it.
There are some variously torn & glued-on envelopes
making irregular pale brown patches. Chiefly, over
& over again, in white, the quarto sheets of paper
— notes — saying 'gone to Anna's', 'gone
to Anna's', so that the collage is a waving delicate white
field of Anna Anna Annas.

*

Cigarettes thrown outside —

                                        The grass, with Vicki

David, & the rest.

                    (I am

stretching / in the chair. The TV

laughs at something quietly; everyone's

love for everyone else in the air

                  *

Mark's eating & the cats won't let him eat his food

"every day I have the blues" we sing.

Ro has insoluble amatory problems, &

Vicki & David keep shouting at each other,

& Kerry says

                    "I feel as though I've been a fool.

I feel as though I've been gypping myself, & gypping

someone else, too."

I've been doing that for a long time, says Vicki.

Mark's gone to bed with his troubles

(his bracelet) but can't sleep

cause we're playing

Miles Davis so loud

— *WE'RE* so blue!

I feel like keeping

56

a vigil tonight, says Kerry sadly, chastely.

"A what?" Vicki says.

                    *

the greenness of the tree is so very green
that in the morning rain it is almost sentimental
saying "health" & "green" & "delicate"

the whiteness of my foot in this light
beautiful brighter & cleaner than even … (?)

Vermeer ?

                        #
            —— carpets, coffee cups, jeans
                    #

                                            outside
the workmen are banging a piece of metal. I cannot
see or know what they are doing. They have been doing
nothing probably they've been talking & sound
friendly. now one of them is hitting some piece of metal
& a sound is ringing out in the street below that is
so beautiful so loud in the silence that what sound
could be more beautiful what sound could be so much
more celebratory & beautiful than any other

                    *

prone, on the bed,
snoring.   the pornography of your thighs
assumes   an otherness & unreality —

Out the window the tiles of the nunnery
stretch continuous. the trees, in the street, are still;
& building-, engineering-sounds, & trucks, hum below the
silence   in the distance,   in the sun

*

a boeing, its wheels hanging below it
                        is climbing
down the glass of the sky, a pale clear blue, behind the
leaves — this is out the window, above the round part
of the building
                        where the old nuns die
                                                even now
I can see a nun in white through the window   washing
stethoscopes

                    some nuns   are laughing in the monastery
but I can't see them, & some nun
must be dying.

The Breughel equation

we go up the stairs — wrought iron,
like the restaurant, a spiral & upstairs her room, vast.
& outside it's beautiful. Dufy. It's the landscape
at Collioure it's Caulfield at least, sending it up,
but it is real — so blue, & the room

is cool why does she like me her pubic hairs are fairly few
or not thick but cover a largish area of her groin I let them
catch on my teeth gently, at first, but less so & her leg
groans & folds over me pressing me close loving the bite
                                    the smell is summer   caramel
the skin   the smell is of heat   & the girl is gorgeous & wants
to fuck   I'm looking over her shoulder at her face, her teeth, on
her stomach   her face becoming the most beautiful
animal's   the muscles
in her shoulder   moving slowly over &
over   the hot smell
coming thicker from her back   fit & supple
I bite it   where I can   the shoulder
every movement she makes
my desire personified   no-person   beautiful ...
   we are she is.   moving on her own now
chasing it

all the grass is seeding & looks
beautiful

immobilises

a huge, dust-motey gold   but no dust motes — just
the gold — has settled on the trees & I feel my body
go golden   in sympathy   it is
the evening. Indeed   soon
                                              a calm / ready
to rush out   & be as active as buggery

but this is dwindling.   blue. & soon everything
will be relaxed   & nothing will have happened

as expected   in the end what does it all matter.

bright & clear & depressing as a Wesselman painting

the day is a dictionary of symbols for the day   explaining
that nearly everything happened on time, that could be expected, &
no more, no other

mystery at noon
is pretty direct   but given that we know it
what name will we give it

though you haven't noticed, the trees are gazing
fixedly, though without attention,
all about them.

a sudden change   has come over it
& makes no difference.

avid
            avidity

a plane, a
boeing   is climbing
down the pale, clear, glass of the sky, at a gradual
silent angle.

              "Winter boats

        are visible in the harbour.
        Dufy."

but quieter. (— *The*
Piano Lesson of Matisse   A child writes
"La pluie."   All noise is engendered
As we sit listening. I lose myself
In other's dreams."

*

"tennis"

*

                                — but out the window it is
real enough. only, the line is a little crisp   like a photo in a glossy
American magazine (an ad for scotch or open-necked
shirts. or golf.
                        inside,
it is dark. it will lighten later
as the light angles in through the windows   opening
on to the little porch   ... outside   the trees are moving a
brilliant green   & above (beyond) the caramel brick of the nuns'
new building.

                    making
the sky seem a darker, more mysterious blue
two telephone wires belly gracefully across, dark,
making it hard to judge the depth behind them, distances.
seeming to shift.   recede, come nearer
till you look away.

— you go outside then.

& nothing.   except that it's
cool. —
a faltering breeze   is touching you,   occasionally

down the street, above the houses, the sky is looking
all blue & oracular   as though a helicopter might appear
& commence firing   or a (giant) wingless angel from Raphael's Bible
& start shouting   all waving limbs & flying cloaks, wasp-like, as though
outside a window-pane & we can't hear him

though you haven't noticed   the trees are gazing   (etc)

constraint;   constrained.

as expected — the physiology of the day: she has
some important news for him

                                                "Her silence
is the James Dean factor"

                                        What to make of this?
is it that "*till he comes* / her silence is the 'James
Dean' factor"?   (A kind of boredom?)   (An
imminent activity?)

Carry me
to the Vermeers, the Diebenkorns, the Gorkys

she wants to live   "in the sky, &
… (like that)"

    she just flew about the room
            in great big curves

I think of the poem again
& *The Music Lesson*

& the child's head from /
the painting — made
 calm, & singular, & precious /
as one piano note: still.

                    *

                    Winter boats
are visible in the harbour   : a sail / as white
as a piano key   in the dark   "La pluie" a child writes
All noise is engendered   as we sit listening

Gary was doing nothing spectacular: dawn, Bondi beach,
swimming naked in the pool.   "How beautiful
to do a realist ad. : not really dawn, but pre-dawn & Gary
swimming way over from the far corner of the pool
& coming up at the side water-faced & saying
'The old bin 23 Riesling basically speaking,' holding up the wine

he & I & Louise had drunk a dozen or so bottles of
this week. Louise—as he swam away,
to the middle of the pool, leaving the bottle behind, the label
facing us (&) slightly torn—Louise standing up
unconcerned about looking beautiful & looking beautiful
squeezing water from her hair."

liking them both   great & ordinary & knowable
as the scene

in an oblique line / across the pool undramatically. the sky
only just getting blue, around its edges, the water in the pool
very dark & windy, & the surf outside is rough, unspectacularly high
& black
                    the cement wall

                                        low   & not modern not
luxurious — rough —   but regular enough to not look natural — one of those
old-fashioned, utilitarian salt water pools cemented on the rocks

Gary goes by not after the rewarding kiss swimming obliquely

"feminine, marvellous & tough" I think
& take a swig — I can't swim. I'm dressed!
 jeans, jumper on my bare skin.

                              & outwards
you may go, or not go, & it doesn't matter   the trees wave
their pointy heads above you   (indicat(ing) nothing
possibly

downstairs

Louise is fucking Gary, outside
the night is making the industrial noises
to which I'm used (quietly, & with
a kind of echo);   I am drunk

& have just decided   that I am winning — on balance, I think —
the fight against self-pity

'a' fight, against self-pity?
                              (*though is* this
what I am feeling?) …

                                        … all over the floor, the drinking
glass   appearing here,   there   & reappearing always,
emptied — refilled

                              & objects,
moving /   from time to time,   perform
a slow, cubist minuet   moving slowly & subtly about the room
the scene   seen always *as* a scene — framed / by the window
or the french doors   or, — the small box —   seen, & recognized,
only when seen again, from that same point of view,
— from which you must have stared at it for some time,
& come to know its details, the way the shadows fall inside it
airless & softening

                    & just where the softness occurs

                              & its 'meaning'

             Thus time becomes a labyrinth
of echos   something physical & unknown   except at its points
& corners   where it "juts out"   ——   these "scenes" its edges,
the corners of the cell it circumscribes   time is met here

                    #

                              that
though — yes — it was less & yet
exactly *like* the story books,
that, though it is almost by the
amount & exactly in the *way*
that he differs, that he does not fit
the standard account, it is
by this that he disappoints her (which is
self knowledge) & yet she loves him & is she
surprised? as geese fly 'overhead' like
a motif representing 'tradition' emphas-
ising 'repetition'   & the *concept*
of a truth thereby, but not / that it is
true   ——   this
simply suggested?)

something she considers

               —— a Chinese girl, in
the reeds, by the river ——
                              does she
touch him, now, looking
away from the sky

66

: unspoken, &, finally, for her benefit,
generosity towards him — a touch
as of / reassurance   while he lies
thinking

                     & stirs slightly   — a
tenderness
for him

(he cannot know

               what she is thinking
               what she has thought)

her hairs,
I let them 'catch on my teeth'
gently at first but less so her leg groans
& folds over me

your skirt higher

takes you & have your nails grown
longer (are they painted?)   as they dig
I love you my heart is saying

            lifts

on the ad on TV the Russian clowns & dancers are depicted
jumping about   The Kapitan is a good German
a real man & human he says *Germany is
making Hitler a machine,* or something.

Robert Mitchum, up above, the boys admire him so,
one of them has lost a hand, he'd've *given*
his hand   to get that U-boat   the dancer with the
smile she's fucking that one she loves him, in their
helmets they look so glamorous. "This
is where we stand," says Bob ('coffee') everyone
is human (ah, 'back home') of the Germans one of them
is misguided   he is probably a nazi. They have just begun to fuck
others in the company know it but no one disapproves:
it's been done before ... separated from the country's
mores : there is the Western influence ... the progressive ideology
of the revolution, in any case — & probably the natural
aristocracy of the profession: meaning independence ... up
above they've been hit Curt Jurgens got him in
the engine room they'll give the Captain all they've got
who can blame them? who will protect
the dance   when it's on, in a few days time? are the dancers
guilty? — at nights despite their tiredness, Yuli & Anna
make love they are happy with their lives

#

your big soft lust lifts
her hairs   catch
on my teeth
takes you   & have your nails grown
gently at first but less so & her leg groans
& folds over me
your skirt higher
longer (& are they painted?) as they dig
"I love you" my heart is saying

going over to Margaret's place
& coming back &
fixing up poems

II

your skirt higher
your lust lifts
longer (& are they painted? red?) as they dig
takes you & have your nails grown ("longer" she said)
"I love you" my heart is saying (her
hairs)   catch
& folds over me
gently at first but less so   her leg groans

the leaves.
As though they really have no meaning   just / rattling
or whispering. & later :   the trees, the wrought iron railing   ...

"... zigzagging his way from the pieties of
tradition to the innovations of the avant-garde & back again;
uncertain, intense, ambitious, intelligent, immensely talented,
& absolutely serious."

I love this stuff

the choice of the title, *luxe, calme & volupté*,
alerts us to
is, in some respects, as significant as the style in
which the painting is executed. It alerts us to

the kind of imaginary paradise that now
begins to beckon from Mrs Matisse's

... vagina?

was it 'sadness' ?   was it sadness & inexplica-
bility, together? & some link between them?

                                        & the blue
reminds me   of a very small porcelain earring I
rediscovered, once,   years after I had last thought of them
— a pair I had   & thought beautiful   & put
in a box

back at the car Neil is looking at the map,
which means that either he will drive or Anna will;
he will say that he will drive *till here* & naming a town, or that
he will *take over* 'from there'. I am watching the steam
rise from the dirt & edge of ragged green grass
from the last of the dregs of the tea where I have thrown it.
In the corner of my eye Nicki is putting out the fire
kicking & scuffing dirt over it with her boots.
We are together perhaps because we had each, at one stage,
represented possibilities for each other; & momentum,
habit, trajectory? has kept us together for this one, last
(?) time. 'Fateful'.   Angela
has gone off for a piss. I join the others at the car.

looking back, without even the

faintest feelings of regret (for we
had felt nothing) we left
the mountains & scorched, quietly,
into the cool flat land
of trees, which moved, green, outside
our windows. & when we got out they
rattled slitheringly even as we had closed
our doors. – us, & the car, & 'the scene'.

                              our isolated phrases
out of place on the ground where we have chosen
for a fire. The women
don't like each other. Anna sits on the
short log available while Nicki stands apart
& looking outward. Neil & I
walk down the slope for the creek.

                    Everyone settles for less.

perhaps I speak for myself.

              a vision of myself
              at 40
              sitting in this restaurant,
              alone. at the other tables
              are all my friends,
              whom I've introduced
              to *Diethnes,* all
              fucking each other, come to eat. this

nearly happened

the other night.   (In this picture I have

of myself I look

exactly like Juan Gris

)

when I got home, after an hour

or so, my old girlfriend

knocked on the door. I ran downstairs

to answer,

in case it was my old girlfriend, "I won't come in,"

she said "if you're just going to sleep." "No!" I said, "No,

come on up!" "You're sure?" "Come on up,"

I said. Up we went. "Your room's changed."

"Yes, it's still nice though,

don't you think?" Yes she said. I said,

soon after, "Would you

like a fuck?" "Yes! alright," she said. "Good.

Good." "How's

life been?" she said. "O, Christ, terrible

I guess. I mean, you know — alright." We said about

two more things each & answered them. "Do you want to get into bed

now?" This made her smile. Standing up we pawed each other

for a while, then went to bed

                                        tunes

                        Muddy Waters :
                        Long Distance Call

                                                Rembetika

72

<u>**When she speaks she makes absolute sense —**</u>
<u>**I am her only weakness.**</u>

coming in, coming 'home'
is a little Fokker Friendship, coming in over the
roofs, a little 'privately-desperately' — like a
cat as it starts to rain, walking-nearly-running, its
ears flattened & back, & its head lowered. In the rainy sky
over the buildings over the road, loveable. I am
reading Frank O'Hara's poems — the *Lunch Poems* —
& wondering   whether my first book …

)))

                    outside
the bruisy, laden sky   & its totally clear &
hurried air, winter trying to begin. And there's the plane
needing sympathy, or evoking it

                                    coming down

& suddenly the girls break out of the school across
            the road
their voices

            (absolving the plane of difficulty)

                    #

            "Here's our old friend, the tetrahedron"
he said, & then I loved him

                        (*unquote*)

*

"And yet,"

*

(to quote again)

*

"With Beethoven the parts of a composition were defined by means
of harmony. With Satie & Webern by
means of time lengths. The question of structure is so basic, &
it is so important to be in agreement about it, that
one must now ask: Was Beethoven right or are Webern
& Satie right? I answer immediately & unequivocally,
Beethoven was in error, & his influence, which has been
as extensive as it is lamentable, has been deadening
to the art of music. ...

          Silence cannot be heard in
terms of pitch or harmony: it is heard in terms of
time length." Cage further went on to say
that Beethoven had practically "shipwrecked"
music "on an island of decadence."

          #

Saw Pie off to Melbourne. Drunk this night, we finally arrived at Bondi beach where
Gary & Louise were going to swim. It was cold. On the other side of the beach, which
curved around on our right as we faced the sea, the lights that edged the wall around
the beach were burning — bright, & phosphorescent, & cold. It was night when we got
there & gradually, by the time we left, had greyed to morning.

I was so in love then & lonely but not in love with anyone or with any one thing just that everything seemed so real then I had to describe it to try to hold it, try to believe it. Everything felt desperately real. *"It was the pathetic fallacy."* (joke)

It was only a little while after that—that Gary & Louise got off together though the affair they began didn't last very long &, after a while, was unhappy for both. This was probably very obviously in the air already. But I didn't notice. October/November, '74. '75 maybe. Everything I saw turned into poems.

                    *

"God moves among the casseroles." (— St Theresa)

                (He's in my Coke!)

"Man is an historical animal."
                            — Stewart Granger

"God *moves* — even — among arseholes."
                            — Lou Reed

        & like a glass added to water
        something useful finds its perfect form

I was frightened to go to sleep again, but I did, & that time it was different.
I dreamed again of the great city by the sea, with its houses & streets, & the
things that flew in the sky. It was years since I had dreamed about that, but
it still looked just the same, & in some quite obscure way it soothed me.
                            The Chrysalids, John Wyndham

The cheesy grin —
of Celeste Holm

                                          the dark bits
& interesting creases where the body gets
more interesting

                — from "Art Book Of The Heart"

        ((**bucolic**))

        little rictus
        describes
        no one. While
        little dithyram
        describes bantam.
        the hen's a big meringue.
        Shirley thinks she's
        very smart going
        fast & being
        still. Butch is
        motionless
        awk awk, scratch,
        blink, leap
        yawn — the circus
        across the lane,
        the children, scream
        where they are minded—

yelling, banging things:
Guernica
"Graeme! Graeme!
Margaret!" You two,
the teacher yells.
BOOM

the animals
are being themselves. Motionlessly,
like the most gently wafting balloon
or as though the air is a very thick
medium, Butch moves
forward. the big white hen
scratches at the earth — a kind of
slow fat matron's hoedown.
Shirley is an emergency, an
insurrection. bantam
is still — he looks a bit too real
to be true, but very convincing.
… spoils it with a little rooster
noise, a cough. unbelievable.

    #

as though love itself were the arsonist

    #

(Love Poem)

not / like a lion, or a pool table or an old-style
bike. & not very much more like all of them together

out of context. a little bit like thinking fleetingly
of a shark, the impulse to write.

                like a tadpole darting
from rock to rock in a pool.

           like night.

II

though it is day (will I go on?)
that I am writing this. the kind of day
you might compare to a hot night — but in
a cliched way, therefore not very precise. now,
beside the lion, who looks very much like Gerald Ford, a fly
must have appeared   something *like* a fly

reading—
on the floor my very soft leather shoes
& Anna's (light) blue &
white thongs. & the house quiet,
& through the floor above us (the
roof) the raucous blues of some crazed
white man, his breath a bit short & the
guitar lines very fast. we're not bored
we're not excited   this is a nice
afternoon. overcast outside. Lying in
bed, in our clothes — the music
thumping, pleasantly, through the roof
has slowed down now. Anna & I
talk briefly about David Miller's story.
we read again. "Why have they done this?" she says quietly, & indicates.
I don't know why. We decide

maybe it's a joke or something on his using parentheses
(the title, repeated, at the top of each page).
                                        "I think
David Miller's good," Anna says.

GRADUALLY

GRADUALLY as
show biz, more gradually than fashion —

gradually
as the Rolling Stones   took up drugs
& their image
came to center upon them,

or as the career of Frank Sinatra
picked up   (I mean this last,
not the first time),

or, as when you attempt to find first, engaging second,
& the car moves very slowly forward

"Judd's, Morris's, Andre's, Steiner's, some but not all of
Smithson's, some but not all of LeWitt's"

                                        this thing happened.

"For every genuine moment in modern sculpture
— such as John Chamberlain's own crushed
automobile sculptures of the mid-fifties — there are

hundreds & hundreds of driftwood vulvas,
cast in bronze, & called *Departure*."

Art Talk Suite, for Neil Moore

Tristesse notes

the tristesse of waitress & usherette & petrol station attendant

Tristesse found its ideal & interpretation—
              found its ideal *interpreter* —   in ... Edward Hopper

                    #

of pump, station, & attendant

                    #

b-b-b-bonjour, Tristesse (Lichtenstein)

the enigma of Zara Tristesse

" — a new mood of exploration has arisen. Artists,
like skuba-divers, don their masks (of meta irony) to explore
the offshore regions of that warm ocean which is at once a
language & the physical world."

#
("Art Talk Suite")
#

the sadness & mystery
of the least bit of wall, or pier, or beach.

intersecting lines
senil gnitcesretni

"little oeuvres"

down the street along the (famous)
walls (by Edward Hopper)

"radically uncertain"

"gliding like surf around the coral reefs of
 philosophy"   —
                    (Bergson's thought ...)

                 #
          (*apparently*)
                 #

       Manet: "Judy, Judy, Judy!"
       Pissarro: "All right you dirty rat."

"No form, no structure," & Cezanne
stood very still. He did it for some time. We watched. From
the corner of his mouth he said, "What am I?"
        "A Mountain!" It was obvious

adult art book of the heart

the moon, the life, & the hands are mine   (Denis Gallagher)

she just flew thru the air in big curves

        have I used that?

wine

                RILKE !

                little oeuvres

Terrific book.
To look at

never
open it

just to
think of it
makes me think of
roses,

The chocolate-
box

of Europe, culture.

Boy!

the terrific sadness

of the least bit
of wall or beer or

peach, sitting here
in Australia

—— As Rudi says, "All these
summers pissed."

I say
"Coonabarabran ——
stays forever on my mind."

a small dark goddess
gets off the bus & crosses the road, pale scarf
black jeans & shirt   I know this girl   what luck

"You look good to me" ——
(Fats Waller, & a film of twenties porn. O,
psychopathology of everyday life!)

in this hour of probable fulfillment!

*

iron bars on the window,
... traffic

*

I have these thoughts
                                    at night
come into my head
                        sort of visitants

hi gang!

*

I give up you,
wonderful idea,
silly idea really —
but *at least I know
how you felt*

(embodied thought)

        I sit up
late at night, try to think —
Of what to say
next
            & after a few phrases —
"Rainer Maria Rilk" (!) — forget myself:
I'm listening to the
waves — crashing down the cliff.
There is something terrific
about this: all this art
in front of me, half finished,
Lou Reed on the record player
but stopped, ages ago, but I could
put it on. And that's the thing,
two pages of cartoons in front of me,
also nearly finished. And this,
my notebook in front of me
filled with things — some bad
& some *beginning to gel* —
from mere scraps of hopelessness: six
months of unfinishedness,
bad starts, odd lines, beginning
to gel some of it — in a
way / I had never intended,
beginning to tell

                              exactly
what my mind had done
                #
but without the awfulness
with charm
                #

                              the grace
of it
                almost makes you laugh
— almost cry —
                        as the tension drains out, the
terribleness of it

it all seems innocent. You
stand up.

                #

                Why isn't there a drink
in the house
                        to spin out
this terrific trance
of the last year 'flowered'
                        so suddenly
so long after time &
                after waiting, its anguish
& form & prayer

anguish? form? prayer??

Yike!

#

I give up you,
silly idea
— wonderful idea, really —

at least I know
how you felt

#

suddenly, his mind went Queensland

                    marijuana alters
                    my mental state,
                    & I go surfing

                    Back home I
                    feel great & I

                    go back to my
                    roots, annotate

                    (all) my Muddy Waters records,

                    then Wolf,
                    & Walter —

& I am made to
feel great too.

alone in the pool
my head sticks up
like a bungled bust of beethoven
ocean on one side, sky above, mountains
ringed around (whatever *that* means —
I should probably say "to my left
the mountains"), a truck shunting down the
hill, plane coming out of cloud
in the far distance, a straight line towards you,
& overhead, (& on to Melbourne)

"If only you could be a girl for a little while
and, moreover, such a peculiar one as I . . ."
— letter, Jenny Von Westphalen to Karl Marx

it's a thought I suppose)

#

the post Leonetti hours   the benevolent blue hum

#

"Allow me love to think a little wildly:
Always I am unhappy, living discretely,

— Louise Labé, 1524 — 66, *The Baroque Poem*

multi beno

'truckie' for "lots of pills"

SUBURBS

free of the brave — land of the home

(QUOTE)

"staying is nowhere" — Rilke, elegy one

is you there, Shelley, a-pantin'?
 She's not here, Man, if you're looking
for her —
And he 'goes off' — looking for
Dark Death, a kind of female Darth
Vader — in harem pants — shouting
Some call her Lilithe, I call her
Tequila! & jumps into his Alfa

An Adamson moment

"O souls of those I've loved, souls of those I've
sung, strengthen & support me, drive falsehood

from me & this world's corrupting
vapours . . .
                  — Baudelaire   (!)

"I walk alone, practising my fantastic fencing" — Baudelaire

      Baudelaire again

          boodle it

               Michael Zerman
               —literally sisterless.

               I am in Adelaide.

The cat butts my chin
a head butter for love

(would you of?)

                    My heart sets out
                       on another one of its trips

Anselm Kiefer

Me, whose task is wakefulness itself   (Nietzsche)

(my little alarm clock)

                          I wake   —

                                                as my
girlfriend comes home
climbs the ladder to the loft

                "gets next to me"

                                we look down & out the window—
                                at the trees blowing there,
                                the footpath & people passing

        Tea — would you like
                a cup?

Notes

Footprints—The CD *Footprints 'live'* revives many of Wayne Shorter's best compositions & adds some new. Here I attempt to do something similar.

London Poem—as it says, idle contemplation of a postcard showing a beautiful young woman looking very overwrought. The Wapping Project is an old water-pumping station adapted as a coffee-&-culture spot. It's nice.

On Reflection—I run a bookshop just off Hindley Street, a part of the Australian Experimental Art Foundation. Klimt's painting *Danae* features briefly, delivering a kind of judgement, in the film of the Henry James novel *The Wings Of A Dove*.

Some Days—composed in 1999 and much worked on, largely from scraps written in the mid to late 70s.

My thanks to the relevant editors for previous publication of

'Footprints' in *JACKET2*;
'The Funnies' in *Best Australian Poems 2011;*
and 'On Reflection' in *Ottoliths*

and my thanks particularly to Pam Brown and Laurie Duggan
for many suggestions along the way